HARES

First published in Great Britain in 1995 by
Colin Baxter Photography Ltd.,
Grantown-on-Spey,
Morayshire, PH26 3NA
Scotland

A CIP Catalogue record for this book is available from the British Library

ISBN 0-948661-28-3

Photographs © 1995:

Front Cover © E. A. James (Nature Photographers)
Back Cover © Keith Ringland
Page 1 © Laurie Campbell
Page 4 © Neil McIntyre
Page 7 © Laurie Campbell
Page 8 © Colin Baxter
Page 10 © Manfred Danegger (NHPA)
Page 11 © Manfred Danegger (NHPA)
Page 12 Left © Neil McIntyre
Page 12 Right © Neil McIntyre
Page 15 © E. A. James (NHPA)
Page 16 © Neil McIntyre
Page 19 Top © Keith Ringland
Page 19 Bottom © John Hayward (NHPA)
Page 21 © T. Kitchin & V. Hurst (NHPA)
Page 23 © Nigel Dennis (NHPA)

Page 24 © Neil McIntyre
Page 25 © Colin Baxter
Page 26 © Laurie Campbell
Page 28 © Manfred Danegger (NHPA)
Page 29 © Niall Benvie
Page 31 © Laurie Campbell
Page 32 © Neil McIntyre
Page 33 © Neil McIntyre
Page 35 © Neil McIntyre
Page 37 © Colin Baxter
Page 38 © Laurie Campbell
Page 39 © E. A. James (NHPA)
Page 40 © Neil McIntyre
Page 43 © Neil McIntyre
Page 44 © E. A. James (NHPA)
Page 47 © Neil McIntyre

Printed in Hong Kong

HARES

Keith Graham

Colin Baxter Photography, Grantown-on-Spey, Scotland

Hares

As surely as Aesop's hare should have outrun its tortoise rival, so, in theory, should a Russian wolf-hound, or Borzoi, outrun a hare. If sheer speed were to represent the be all and end all of the chase, then the hare, whilst able to outrun most predators, would always perish if pursued by such a speedy dog.

Anna was one such dog. Pampered though she may have been, she was nevertheless lean, fit and raring to go. Rabbits were certainly no match for her; their blind, panic-stricken and direct bolts for cover made them easy prey. Hares were different.

There is no hunting purpose in my gentle perambulation through the fields, yet, for Anna always, the starting gun is raised and ready to catapult her into action. She lifts her nose to the wind, sifting it for the slightest trace of scent which might instantly focus her mind upon the very talents which generations of careful breeding have prepared her for. She is like a coiled spring, ready to stretch her long legs in swift pursuit. Thirty yards away – no more – crouched in the shallowest of depressions, ears laid flat over his neck and upper back, the jack hare waits and wonders. His instincts tell him, as they have told him a thousand times before, that to remain motionless may be his best defence. His nostrils too are twitching and sifting; his eyes, set high on the sides of his narrow head, give him global vision – he watches and waits.

He believes himself to be invisible even if, with his monochrome vision, he cannot except by instinct know that his brindly brown coat

A mountain hare crouched in heather.

mixes well with the background of a winter-browned, molehill-marked field of grass.

But there is a frontier of tolerance, a frontier invisible but intuitively calculated; by crossing it a threatening predator demands and prompts different tactics. Anna has crossed that line and impulsively he is up and running. The hare's movement is the starting pistol she has been waiting for. Suddenly her long legs are digging deep for instant speed, her head low and pointing inexorably towards that loping, escaping brown figure.

His initial flight is not swift and he cruises on stiff legs, ears upright, head held high. The gap between huntress and hunted is rapidly narrowing as Anna hits full throttle. Although he too now accelerates smoothly, the odds on his survival seem to be narrowing with each ground-consuming stride as her long legs eat up the space between them. Anna is nearly upon him when he also digs deep into his energy resources, legs pumping. The hare's ears go back and he employs a slight change of course, first to the left and then to the right, before abruptly and without warning altering direction completely, turning sharp left.

This instant turn, engaged by the sudden thrust and twist of his long and powerful hind legs, takes him at right angles to his original course, just as Anna was closing in, her eager and gaping carnivore's mouth no more than a tantalising foot or two from his rump. The shock of his turn gives him instant freedom. Anna may be fast but such a turn is beyond her. As he slows to that stiff-legged cruise again, and makes confidently for a familiar gap in the hedge, she careers on and on, tail winding in a frantic and futile effort to apply the brakes. She has lost; he has won. It was a 'no contest' from the start, for despite her superior speed, and not many can claim that advantage over a brown hare, his athleticism and tactical know-

The courtship of brown hares (Lepus europaeus) is most obvious in the months of February and March but they are capable of producing three litters of youngsters in a year. Later bouts of courtship are more subdued and lack the displays of eccentric behaviour so typical in the Spring.

Mountain hares frequently dig short burrows or snow holes in which to shelter from the worst of the weather. The white winter coat provides excellent camouflage on the hillsides during the Winter months when these animals are relatively easy to approach.

how have left Anna vainly casting around for the sight and scent of her prey. By the time she has returned, panting and frustrated, to the spot where her quarry was last within sight, he is long gone.

I have never witnessed the ancient field sport of hare-coursing, but can imagine that it is a thrilling spectacle. I have never been a supporter of the hunt, and certainly question its very raison d'être. I am, however, well aware that modern hare-coursing is organised in such a way as to narrow the odds in favour of the dogs with dog-handlers, with spectators aligning the sides of the arena field, leaving the hares little choice but to try and outrun the dogs in their attempt to reach safety.

Countless generations of hares have by the very nature of things been the object of pursuit by man, his hounds and his horses for perhaps longer than any other creature in the United Kingdom. The hare — the gentle, soft-eyed hare — has unquestionably and historically always been a prized quarry, be it by the hunt as it has been practised by man, or the hunt as it is lived every day in nature by bird and beast.

Beagling, a pastime still popular in some areas, particularly in the southern half of England, has a long tradition, even longer perhaps than that of fox hunting, the difference of course is that the hounds are followed on foot rather than horseback. Beagles, short in the leg but otherwise similar to fox hounds, are not particularly speedy animals but they are dogged in their ability to patiently follow a scent trail. Hares benefit from having plenty of stamina, but it is a characteristic of beagles that they too are indefatigable, their objective becoming one of literally wearing down their quarry.

The hare-shoot has also long been a popular sporting tradition. The game records of some country estates show substantial bags from years past. Currently such shoots are less popular than they once were, although on parts of the Continent hare-shoots are still very much a part of the sporting calendar.

Today, perhaps because their numbers have declined and perhaps because there are more prestigious quarries to pursue, such as stags and grouse, the hare has been relegated to a minor role in the area of field sports. It may also be, of course, that public opinion makes such pastimes unacceptable. To some degree, the ethics of conservation have overtaken the ethos of the hunt.

Two young brown hare leverets crouching in a meadow.

Our own perception of hares is generally rooted in those glimpses we have of them careering blindly in front of our cars, zig-zagging on impulse and by instinct in a vain effort to throw off the glaring, noisy, and all too swift a pursuer. Those eyes, with vision which serves the hare so well against most predators, fail it when the brilliant lights of a vehicle blind it to escape routes. Nothing is more successful when set against the hare than the modern motor vehicle. The evidence is all too obvious in the litter of carcasses upon our tarmac roads.

A brown hare doe (opposite) suckling two of her leverets.

These pictures show the typical running movement of the
mountain hare across a snowfield. The broad feet which have hair on the soles,
act like snow-shoes to give surer footing. This animal is not hurrying but it is
capable of considerable speed when pursued by a predator.

Perhaps our vision of hares is coloured by the spectacle of speed – the sight of a hare loping easily, but swiftly across an open field. Yet again, we may have identified them as brown humps amongst the growing crops as they patiently nibble away at the vegetation. Hill-walkers may know the mountain hares as blue shadows amongst the snow-covered hummocks of high places, almost to be stood upon before they will move. And there are those fortunate people who have watched the cavorting – the mad-Marching – of hares during that one and only period in their yearly life-cycle when they appear to be possessed by devils, throwing aside their shyness and singularity to become community orientated, aggressive or just plain daft. In the Spring of the year, you can now see that other essential side of the coin as the jacks compete with each other for the right to procreate: fighting; jumping; leaping; biting; scratching and kicking.

But the action is not entirely the province of the males, for each jill too, will physically resist even the most ardent approach of competing males until she is absolutely ready to receive them. Until that instinctive moment is reached, she will also rear on her hind legs, boxing and cajoling her suitors. She will leap away from, and even over, an over-ambitious, pursuing male.

Such is the contradictory lifestyle of this enchanting, yet mysterious creature about which we know comparatively little, albeit that it is instantly recognisable from occasional brief glimpses – and, of course, from those legendary races with tortoises.

Hares, together with rabbits which they closely resemble, and pikas which they do not, are classified as members of the lagomorphs. A comparatively small family, it is distinguished by the zoologist from the rodents by the presence of an extra pair of small teeth situated behind the large incisors. One other feature, in this case behavioural, sets them apart. Hares, like rabbits, increase the efficiency of digestion by refection, a method of recycling the cellulose-rich food which is their diet. In other words, they eat their own droppings in order to fully utilise nutrients which, because the cellulose is so difficult to digest, pass through the system unused.

Pikas, of which there are more than a dozen species, found in parts of Asia and North America, are hamster-like creatures with short legs and small, rounded ears. In physical appearance, this distinguishes them from rabbits and hares, both of which are identified by their relatively long ears and their longer hind legs. In the case of the hare, the hind legs are exceptionally long.

There is, therefore, a broad physical similarity between rabbits and hares. Equally however, there are many distinctive differences. The rabbit which incidentally is a relatively recent addition to the fauna of Britain, probably having been introduced shortly before the Norman conquest in 1066 and originally a native of southern Europe, is a close, community orientated animal. The hare, by and large, is not. Generally, the rabbit chooses to make its home in burrows where its young are born naked and blind. Conversely, the hare lives mainly above ground (although the mountain hare is known to excavate short burrows). Young are born fully furred and with their eyes open. They are fairly mobile from the start, and are usually independent of their parents within a mere four weeks.

The response to threat is also, and quite naturally, different. A rabbit will bolt on fast-running legs for the nearest burrow. The hare relies on its

A typical pose by a brown hare, photographed in a Lowland meadow.

A mountain hare in Summer. Stockier and with shorter ears than the brown hare,
although the coloration in the Summer months is similar, the mountain hare always has that greyer tinge
and the top of its tail remains white whereas the top of the brown hare's tail is black.

speed (in excess of 45 miles an hour at full bore), its ability to change direction quickly and, in the older animal, upon its wisdom, experience and an intimate knowledge of its territory.

The bobbing white scuts of rabbits are familiar to almost everyone. The short tail of the rabbit is raised when it is fleeing, revealing the white underpart which acts as a warning signal to the rest of the rabbit community in much the same way as the white posterior of a roe deer also alerts each family group to the presence of danger. A hare's tail is similarly white underneath, and in the case of the brown hare, almost black on the upper side, but when the animal is put to flight, the tail remains down. Presumably this is because the hare's more independent existence has left it without the impulse to warn other hares of danger.

There is also a substantial difference in size between the rabbit and the brown hare. The average brown hare is roughly twice the weight of a rabbit with a mature female brown hare weighing as much as eight and one-half pounds compared with the four and one-half of fully-grown rabbit. On average, hare does are generally a little larger than bucks.

When it comes to colour, there is a further division to be made. In Britain there are two very distinctive races of hare – the brown hare (*Lepus europaeus*) and the mountain hare (*Lepus timidus scoticus*). In addition there is also the Irish hare (*Lepus timidus hibernicus*), usually classified with the mountain hare, albeit that this resident of the Gulf Stream-warmed Emerald Isle, seldom, if ever, changes its coat to white in the Winter months. The Irish hare is found at all altitudes, and is generally marginally sturdier and heavier than his Scottish counterpart.

Further confusion can arise from the fact that the mountain hare is also variously known as the 'blue' hare, the 'variable' hare and, particularly in Scotland, as the 'mawkin'. Resident in England, Scotland and Wales, the most obvious distinguishing feature of the mountain hare is that it has the ability to change its coat to white in the Winter months, clearly a means of camouflage in the high mountainous conditions in which it generally lives, but perhaps also an aid to conserving body heat.

In practice, the camouflaging effect is often negated by the hare's need for food. Although it will do this by scraping through the snow, it is clearly easier to find areas where the snow has been blown away from the vegetation, and, in such circumstances, the creature, far from being hidden, is instead exposed.

This ability to change colours according to the season is shared by stoats, and, in the avian world, by the companions of mountain hares in the high places, ptarmigan. The weasel also moults to white in some parts of northern Europe, but not, it seems, in the British Isles.

It was once believed that falling temperatures acted as the stimulus for the change in coat colour to white. Scientific studies have now dismissed that belief in favour of a firm opinion that the shortening hours of daylight in the early Winter act as the trigger. Similarly, the lengthening daylight hours in the Spring stimulate the reversal to the bluish-brown coat of that season. Nevertheless, temperature may have its part to play in the process, especially as the Irish hare, living in a milder gulf-stream warmed climate appears to have abandoned the process altogether. However, this metamorphism is undoubtedly bound up in genetic selection and in Ireland, it is likely that the genetic pool has undergone adjustment in isolation.

Mountain hares are distributed throughout the Palaearctic regions of the northern hemisphere, but there are populations which reach as far

Closely related to the mountain hare, the Irish hare
(Lepus timidus hibernicus) *seldom if ever turns white in the Winter months.*

south as the Alps. Nearer to home, deliberate introductions by man confuse the picture. Although originally confined to the Highlands of Scotland, they are now found in parts of the Lowlands, in the Hebrides, in Shetland and on the island of Hoy in Orkney, the northern Pennines, north Wales and the Peak District of Derbyshire. The Welsh population seems to have slumped in recent years.

Scientists also link the mountain hare as we know it, to the Snowshoe Rabbit (*Lepus americanus*) of North America, sometimes also known as the 'varying' hare. There are no fewer than 16 sub-species represented throughout the world.

The distribution of the brown hare is a little more difficult to pin down owing to the presence of two very similar animals, our own familiar brown hare (*Lepus europaeus*) and the almost identical African Cape hare (*Lepus capensis*) which is also present in Europe, notably in the Iberian peninsula.

The brown hare has a considerable range extending south as far as southern Africa. Its range also stretches from the Arctic regions of the north, across Europe and into western Asia. To add to the confusion, the brown hare of our open fields has also been introduced to Scandinavia (where it was previously absent), to Australia, New Zealand, North and South America, presumably in each case as a hunting quarry.

One of the British introductions to the Calf of Man, a small island lying off the southern tip of the Isle of Man, presents an interesting study of the relationship between rabbit and hare populations. Here it seems that rabbits and hares don't mix well. At the time of the introduction the Calf of Man was swarming with rabbits and the hares eventually disappeared. Evidence would suggest that the aggression of the rabbits was too much

Often known as the Snowshoe Rabbit (Lepus americanus), this resident of North America is in reality, a hare, distinguished from the rabbit by the much greater size of its heart and the bigger volume of blood contained in the body of all hares. There are 52 species of rabbits and hares in the world. Many so called rabbits (including 'Brer Rabbit') are in fact hares.

for the hares, which, despite their superior size, were simply unable to compete for the available food. Of course, there may have been other factors such as disease which could have caused the extinction of the hares.

It is said that hares can be afflicted by myxomatosis, that great scourge of rabbit populations, although there is scant evidence of this. But hares are vulnerable to other diseases, and the contagious infection coccidiosis in particular, is known to pose them a serious problem.

In the British Isles, the brown hare would historically appear to have been very widely distributed, even at relatively high altitudes (up to 2,000ft). Not surprisingly, there has been a decline in numbers in many rural areas which have become urbanised. If the fox, badger, stoat and weasel have, to varying degrees, adapted to the changed environment, the brown hare has not.

Changes in agricultural practices have probably contributed largely to the general decline of brown hare numbers in the British countryside. In my own experience, as recently as 15 years ago, the population in central Scotland was such that one could seldom look out across the fields without expecting to see several hares either loping across the fields or crouching as they fed.

A decade and a half later, and such sightings are nothing as commonplace. The heavy use of chemicals has been cited as one of the reasons for a sharp drop in the hare population, possibly none more deadly than the fast-acting paraquat-based weed killers. Hare shoots, which were popular in this region in the past, may have wreaked some havoc, but generally, wildlife populations are capable of rapid recovery providing there is a sensibly applied control.

*The Cape hare (Lepus capensis) is a resident of Africa and some
southern European countries, and closely resembles its near relative, the brown hare.*

That numbers continued to plummet during the past decade may also have much to do with the switching of emphasis from hay to silage in many parts of lowland Britain, and the advent of fast cutting machinery. Silage making often begins at the time when leverets are very young, and there can be little doubt that this had a deleterious effect upon brown hare populations. It may be concluded that there is heavy mortality amongst young leverets during silage-making operations.

A budding swing away from high levels of intensive agricultural production, and the considerable reduction in the quantity of chemicals now applied to the arable areas (a reduction based partially upon the harsh realities of modern day farming economics, and partially upon curbs on

A brown hare…always on the alert.

production) may at last provide breathing space for the brown hare. Add to this the increasing emphasis now placed upon conservation which is so evident, and it may be surmised that there now exists a climate in which the brown hare can once again prosper. There can be no doubt that some local numbers are on the increase again, even if the overall populations have, as yet, by no means fully recovered. And as land is 'set aside' under European agricultural policy, and thus not effectively farmed in a

Nature's art of obfuscation. Here a mountain hare, dressed in
its Summer coat, illustrates how well it merges with the background of a ploughed
upland field. Sometimes, even the camouflaged hare can be caught out
by early snow storms or, in the Winter, by a lack of snow.

productive sense, wildlife in general is given a little more space and opportunity. Hopefully the brown hare, because it is a creature of open space, will be one of the main beneficiaries of the changing face of farming as we approach the next millennium.

When the lifestyle of the hare is investigated, attention focuses upon Spring when activity is seen very obviously to intensify. In general, the fields are relatively bare of sheltering crops at that time of the year, and the antics which accompany courtship are, thus, very easy to observe. But although sexual activity peaks in March, courtship may begin as early as January. The 'boxing matches' in which hares are seen to rear up on their hind legs, punching each other with their relatively short front legs, is only a part of the courtship ritual which also includes frantic chases with animals leaping over one another, kicking and even biting, sometimes to telling effect.

A brown hare has very powerful hind legs which are strongly clawed. An adversary receiving a raking kick from a rival buck can sometimes be severely and even mortally wounded. It has long been supposed that such behaviour represented competition between males, in short, fighting to establish dominance and so the right to mate. Whilst in part this is true, close observation of hares shows that females also indulge in boxing and leaping. Often a single female will be pursued by a group of enthusiastic males, and, from time to time, she will turn and box with one or more of her pursuers.

Female and male hares are both highly promiscuous. Large, well-established mature bucks it appears, get the choice of the does, and

A close-up of 'Puss', a colloquialism possibly related to the split upper lip.

couple with as many as they can, a clear demonstration of natural selection and the survival of the fittest.

The ritual of courtship appears to so pre-occupy the participants that it is possible at this time of the year to get much closer to what are otherwise shy, retiring creatures with a natural suspicion of man.

Dispersal follows this frenetic period, and soon the animals revert back to a more solitary lifestyle. It could never be said of brown hares that they live in highly structured communities, but in good feeding areas, they do live in loosely assembled groups.

Many 'boxing matches' are promoted by the does.

Brown hare activity is certainly at a peak during the hours of darkness, and at dusk and dawn. In fact, this is the case with most of our native mammals. That is not to say that brown hares are altogether inactive during the hours of daylight, but generally, they are sedentary, typically lying up in their form.

The method of returning to the form or couch after a night's activity also underlines the naturally cautious instinct of a creature, which, one way or another, is pursued rather than the pursuer. Seldom if ever, will a hare return directly to its usual resting place. Instead, a devious route is followed with the animal frequently doubling back on its own trail. There

Brown hares cavorting in the 'mad' month of March. Here, several males are
following a single female (on the extreme right), who is about to physically resist their advances.

is a natural awareness that a scent can be fatally betraying, and hares quite deliberately leap to one side, often clearing considerable distances, in order to break the trail. If predators are seen to be cunning beasts, then cunning is also part of the defence mechanism of the prey.

As evening approaches, a favoured field may appear to almost come alive with hares emerging from their forms and beginning to feed. A doe nursing young will visit each of her leverets in turn to suckle and clean them; it is said that such visits occur only once every 24 hours, generally shortly after dusk.

Such is the fecundity of hares that does can couple almost immediately after giving birth. Indeed, there have been some remarkable examples of does becoming pregnant again even before producing a litter. There are many recorded cases of does having been shot which, upon examination, have revealed embryos at very different stages of development within the womb. As there is no real evidence of pair-bonding, the question arises as to why a second bout of courtship behaviour is not evident in May or June when most does are once again ready to receive the attention of males.

Scientific observation confirms that following the March ritual, virtually 100% of females above a year old are pregnant. In the following months, the percentage of pregnant does reduces, and as the year progresses so the figure continues to decline.

This suggests that further pregnancies occur without the animals resorting to the elaborate courtship ritual so apparent in March. Doubtless, there is some renewed competition between males to mate with an ovulating female, although perhaps more hidden from view because of the early season growth, it is observed less often. The scent

This mountain hare is in a transitional coat, losing its grey-blue Summer colour.
This change is probably influenced more by the shortening days of Autumn and early Winter,
than by temperature. Sometimes, however, the full change does not take place
and some mountain hares remain 'piebald' through the Winter.

A typical gathering of mountain hares, which are
much more gregarious than their brown cousins and often seen in particularly
large numbers. However, this procession may indicate the first stirrings of the breeding
season which approaches in the Spring (above). A profusion of their tracks on a
Scottish mountainside signifies an abundant population (opposite).

emitted by the females, of course, remains the stimulus, but mating can be more a matter of chance after Spring, with neighbouring bucks responding to the inviting scent of ovulating does, providing they are in the right place at the right time.

This lends added credence to the fact that hares do not lead as solitary a lifestyle as was previously thought. Undoubtedly, although hare society can by no stretch of the imagination be described as highly structured, there can be little doubt that bucks live in loose communities with companions of both sexes, and almost always within easy reach of ovulating females.

Three or four litters in a year is probably the average for a mature doe, and births well into the Autumn have been recorded. Weather, inevitably, has a part to play, and Indian summers often result in a further surge in brown hare pregnancies late in the year. So whilst hares cannot compete with rabbits for fecundity, they, nonetheless, exhibit a considerable capacity of fertility.

About 42 days after mating, the doe gives birth to her litter of leverets, born with their eyes open and with a good coat of fur. They are born in a 'form', a depression in the ground created either naturally or partly excavated by the adult animal, but within the first few days of their lives; the youngsters are carefully dispersed to other forms, the doe carrying them by the back of the neck just as a cat carries her kittens. The move, of course, is a precautionary measure which maximises the chances of survival.

Although leverets become independent relatively quickly, initially they do command a great deal of devotion on the part of the does. There have been countless recorded incidents of the bravery and courage exhibited by jills in defence of their leverets. Rural folklore sometimes clouds our judgement in these areas, but without question, does are known to defend their young against attack by foxes and stoats. Stories abound of hares killing stoats using their powerful hind legs to kick. Again, the presence of a sharp set of claws on their feet will have been a contributory factor in at least some of these cases. The jack hares are quite oblivious to the need for any family responsibilities.

My own observation of this devotion to duty is perhaps more mundane, and involved the sight of a jill standing upon her hind legs and very deliberately boxing the nose of a grazing cow which had come too close for comfort to the form in which one of her young leverets rested.

The mountain hare's ear tips remain black year-round.

Whilst an adult hare is easily able to outrun a fox, leverets are vulnerable to predation by foxes. The defence of freezing and remaining in the chosen form is instinctive in the leveret. On several occasions, I have been able to examine a leveret at close quarters in this way, but I do advise against handling them. The presence of an alien scent (and you can't get much more alien than man) may induce the doe to desert a youngster. This rule applies to all wild young mammals.

Although leverets apparently have very little in the way of scent, prowling foxes and stoats, and even the minuscule weasel, will make short work of a young and defenceless 'kitten'. As a result, there is a high mortality rate amongst leverets during the first few days and weeks of their lives until they have accumulated sufficient wisdom and fieldcraft to avoid capture.

The fox appears to register highest on the list of predators against which the hare must guard. Everyone views the fox as a well-honed hunter, perhaps without realising that foxes, above all else, are opportunists and scavengers. Foxes are not averse to patrolling roadsides and dining on the remains of hares. This almost certainly accounts in part for the high number of hare carcasses found in fox dens.

Road victims are, of course, easy meat for them and for other creatures. I well remember being somewhat nonplussed at the sight of the body of a squashed hare twitching on a quiet hill road, only to discover when I approached that a weasel was frantically tugging at one of the legs in a vain effort to remove from the tarmac, a carcass which must have been many times its own weight.

In occupying quite high territories, brown hares also fall victim to eagles, and, indeed, in many Highland glens, probably constitute an important part of the eagle's diet, as does the mountain hare.

In general, mountain hares appear to be slightly more community orientated that their lowland cousins. This 'herding' trait has, of course, been noted in other Arctic-based mammals. Some glens in the Highlands hold very substantial colonies, and they can often be scattered across the hillsides, especially when a rapid thaw clears the ground of snow exposing most manifestly the grazing white hares, not only to the gaze of observant

Brown hares are often seen at quite high altitudes
where their range may occasionally overlap with that of the mountain hare.
Decidedly bigger, with longer ears, the brown hare is much more
'spindly' and less compact than its mountain relative.

The camouflage provided by the winter white coat of the mountain hare sometimes
works in reverse, especially when parts of the hill are cleared of snow in thaws or by the wind. The hares
are automatically attracted to such clear areas where food is more accessible but they are,
in such circumstances, more vulnerable to predation, particularly by eagles.

hill-walkers, but also to cruising keen-eyed eagles. Otherwise, the general behavioural patterns of the mountain hare does not differ substantially from that of the brown hare. Sexual activity is similarly at a peak during the Spring months of March and April, and cavorting mountain hares make just as much a spectacle of themselves during courtship as their brown hare counterparts. However, not surprisingly, the breeding season is shorter. Whereas brown hares will breed into the Autumn, mountain hares seldom produce young after August. And the population of mountain hares appears to be more subject to wild fluctuations, another corre-lation with other Arctic based prey species.

If the brown hare has a fairly general diet ranging from agricultural crops, grasses, hedgerow plants and

A brown hare ambles through a field during Summer.

fungi, to the bark of trees, the mountain hare, by the very nature of hill vegetation, is naturally more restricted in its eating, to ling, cotton and other hill grasses. Soft rushes and gorse are especially important in snowy conditions, but lichens and occasionally conifer cones are also consumed. As with brown hares, refection is a part of the animal's need to maximise the use of cellulose material.

And if brown hares are vulnerable to fox predation, so too are

mountain hares. But also ranged against them are wild cats, and, particularly where the young are concerned, buzzards as well as eagles take their toll.

The timid hare must be ever watchful, and reliant upon its acute sense of smell, sight and, perhaps their keenest faculty, hearing. Curiously, hares seem to be fascinated by loud noise. For example, they are known to gather in groups and increase their activity during thunderstorms. Even more peculiar is an apparent liking for airfields. It would be quite reasonable to presume that the loud, even deafening noise made by the modern jet would be stressful to the hare, but on the contrary, many airports have substantial populations of hares, not just in the peripheral areas, but also in close proximity to runways. On several occasions, at airfields in various parts of this country and on the Continent, I have observed hares cavorting close to taxiing aircraft and beside runways on which jet aircraft were taking-off and landing.

Common sense, of course, deduces that airports have large quantities of grass and herbs upon which the hares can feast unmolested and free from the competition of domestic grazing animals such as sheep. Such places may also be relatively free of predators, but there would seem to be more to it than that. Hares appear somehow to be fascinated by the roar of jet engines. Indeed, some observers have suggested that hares actually enjoy the noise and surmise that the vibrations created by the engines, in some way, and rather like claps of thunder, provide the animals with an enjoyable experience. Such a theory might seem to fly in the face of all reason, but there are so many observations of this kind of behaviour,

A mountain hare changing between its Winter and Summer coats.

coming from a variety of sources that no alternative explanation, as yet, can be found.

Historically, and in contrast to its familiar role of quarry, the hare has long been celebrated in literature and art – it is a familiar subject of cave drawings – lauded as a worthy opponent, even, it would appear, deified. It has been, revered, worshipped as a God, but above all, it has been hunted. That, it seems, is the destiny of the hare.

So gentle is its disposition, so apparently lacking in aggression, so soft and alluring is its gaze, that even its masculinity has been questioned. Some of our forebears were convinced that all hares were essentially feminine, and that even buck or jack hares, – the female, strictly speaking, is a doe although often referred to as a jill – in spite of being possessed of all the necessary male accoutrements, were nevertheless capable of bearing young! This curious belief stems from an old myth which claimed that when the animals departed from Noah's Ark at the end of the great flood, the doe hare had the misfortune to fall in the water and drown. God, thus gave the buck the ability to give birth.

Shakespeare regarded the hare as a melancholy creature, but there is also something vaguely comical about its behaviour. Watch a hare bound across a field, suddenly stop and rear up on its hind legs with its ears erect and its nostrils carefully sifting the air for alien scents, then crouch to nibble at the vegetation and then lope off again, sometimes in a different direction, only to stop once more, and it is easy to get the feeling that this is a somewhat disorganised animal. Yet the hare is a creature of habit. It will use the same trail time and time again. A wise hare is one that has an intimate knowledge of its territory, and most adult hares are wise in the extreme.

A mountain hare only partly sheltered from the storm, its coat matted with driven snow.
When the going gets really tough, mountain hares will descend and seek out shelter and food in plantations.
Apart from camouflage, the winter white also helps to keep the body temperature up.

Two brown hares seemingly getting to know each other. After the hectic episodes of courtship in the Spring, later pairings are more sedate and although hares are relatively solitary, many males stay in reasonable proximity to the does throughout the Summer and are quick to react when they start to ovulate again.

The apparently aberrant behaviour which is so typical of the hare, lay at the heart of Aesop's famous fable about the hare and the tortoise. The moral of that story was that the tortoise, plodding and slow, simply kept going whilst the hare, speedier though it was, was nevertheless erratic, kept stopping and was easily diverted from its course.

Greeks, Romans, Persians, Africans and native American Indians have all given the hare an important place in their folklore. In literature, one of the most touching poems about a hare, incredibly entitled, *On Seeing A Wounded Hare Limp By Me, Which A Fellow Had Just Shot At* was written by Robert Burns.

'Puss', is a frequently used colloquial name for the hare, which some say derives from the Latin, *Lepus*. However, long before Latin was used as the universal language for biological classification, the Greeks also referred to the hare as Puss. Others claim that this name is merely a link to the rural usage of 'kittens' for its young, or even originates from its split upper lip which is somewhat reminiscent of a cat's face.

Whatever nomenclature you prefer, the fact remains that the hare is a curious mixture of many characteristics. It is not noted for vocalisation, generally remaining silent except when screaming terribly in distress or when grinding its teeth in an apparent warning of danger to other hares. Sometimes in courtship it utters grunts, and a doe will make a sucking sound as a warning to its leverets. Generally, it goes about its daily life anonymously and virtually silent.

A hare may start up suddenly or it may lay low, it may fly like the wind or lope across the ground, and, of course, it will walk as it feeds, a curious and clumsy walk which results from the disproportionate size of its front and hind legs.

Yet who would deny that the brown hare, its grey and brown back, ruddy shoulders, neck and flanks, its creamy white underparts, black and white whiskers, wide-open eyes set high on the sides of its head, and its mountain-dwelling counterpart, white-clad in the Winter but otherwise greyish-blue, have not always been a part of the British landscape — highland or lowland — since long before man's arrival here.

And who would deny them a place in the ecology of this land for evermore, employing their speed and fieldcraft in an effort to escape the fox, eagle, cat, and, of course, man, in the age-old struggle for survival.

Hares are ever alert to potential dangers.

Hare Facts

Brown Hare (*Lepus europaeus*)

Size: Average length – 24in (610cm). Average weight – 8lbs (3.5kg).

Appearance: More prominent black hairs give the coat a coarser appearance than that of the rabbit. The underside of the body is white, cheeks, the inside of limbs and feet are redder, sometimes almost yellow. The ears are black-tipped and the top of the tail is black and white underneath. The winter coat is often redder. Moults take place in late Summer/early Autumn and during Spring.

Habitat: Open country to an altitude of 2,000ft but sometimes rest during the day in woodland fringes. More active by night (peak activity sunset-midnight). Present throughout mainland Britain and some islands.

Breeding: Courtship begins in January. Peak of sexual activity is in March. Gestation is approximately 42 days with the average litter size being three or four, with between three and four litters per year. Females first breed at one year of age. Young are born with their eyes open and fully furred.

Food: Vegetarian. Agricultural crops (cereals and grass), turnips, shrubs, tree-bark. Digestive process of refection (eating own droppings).

Relationship with Man: A prized hunting quarry for both beagle packs and hare-coursing, and for shooting. Has been kept in enclosures where breeding takes place in the right conditions. A source of food, the meat is strongly flavoured (like game) and not widely popular. Fur was used in felting.

Mountain Hare (*Lepus timidus scoticus* and *Lepus timidus hibernicus*)

Size: Average length – 20in (500cm). Average weight – 7-8lbs (3.5kg)

Appearance: Stockier than the brown hare with a proportionately larger head but smaller ears. The Summer coat is greyish-brown (blue) with white underparts, black ear tips and a white top to the tail. Moults in the Autumn and again at the onset of Winter when the white pelage appears. However, the ear tips remain black. Reverts to brown in the Spring.

Habitat: Usually found at altitudes up to 4,000ft, mostly in upland areas but some colonies occupy low ground to which they may have been introduced. Present in upland mainland Scotland, Hebrides, Shetland, Orkney, (Hoy), northern Pennines, Peak District and North Wales. Irish sub-species throughout mainland Ireland.

Breeding: Courtship begins February. Peak of sexual activity is in March and early April. Gestation is approximately 45 days with the average litter size three or four, with between three and four litters per year. Young are born with their eyes open and fully furred.

Food: Diet restricted due to habitat; mainly ling, cotton, and other hill grasses, lichens, gorse and soft rushes, occasionally conifer cones. Digestive process of refection (eating own droppings).

Relationship with Man: Extensively shot in parts of the Scottish Highlands. Not important as a food source. Much more approachable than the brown hare.

Bibliography

Burton, Maurice D. Sc., *Wild Animals of the British Isles*, Frederick Warne & Co Ltd., 1968

Evans, George Ewart & Thomson, David, *The Leaping Hare*, Faber and Faber Limited, 1972

Freethy, Ron, *Man And Beast*, Blandford Press, 1983

Southern, R. N., *The Handbook of British Mammals*, Blackwell Scientific Publications, 1964

Tegner, Henry, *Wild Hares*, John Baker (Publishers) Ltd, 1969

Biographical Notes

Naturalist, writer and broadcaster, Keith Graham has enjoyed a life-long love affair with wildlife. The piecing together of the intricate web of nature, understanding its complexities, the inter-relationships and the behavioural patterns of birds and animals especially, is a fatal attraction for him.

He has enjoyed many intriguing encounters with many different birds and animals and through his books, his regular columns and popular slide shows, he always strives to share his knowledge with others and create an empathy with his subjects.

This is the second book he has written in this series. In contrast to hares, creatures which, through the ages, have been prized quarries, his first book concerned one of nature's most renowned hunters, the fox.

This book belongs to:

- -

For Nathaniel Brunner – an inspirational knight,
in memory of his wonderful mum, Cat Johnson. With love. X
K.S.

*Sir Charlie Stinky Socks would like to donate 10% of the royalties from
the sale of this book to Naomi House Children's Hospice.*

EGMONT
We bring stories to life

First published in Great Britain 2013
by Egmont UK Limited
This edition published 2015
The Yellow Building, 1 Nicholas Road
London W11 4AN

www.egmont.co.uk

Text and illustrations copyright © Kristina Stephenson 2013
All rights reserved
Kristina Stephenson has asserted her moral rights

ISBN (PB) 978 1 4052 7773 0

A CIP catalogue record for this title
is available from the British Library

MIX
Paper from
responsible sources
FSC
www.fsc.org
FSC® C018306

THE TALE OF The WIZARD'S WHISPER

Kristina Stephenson

EGMONT

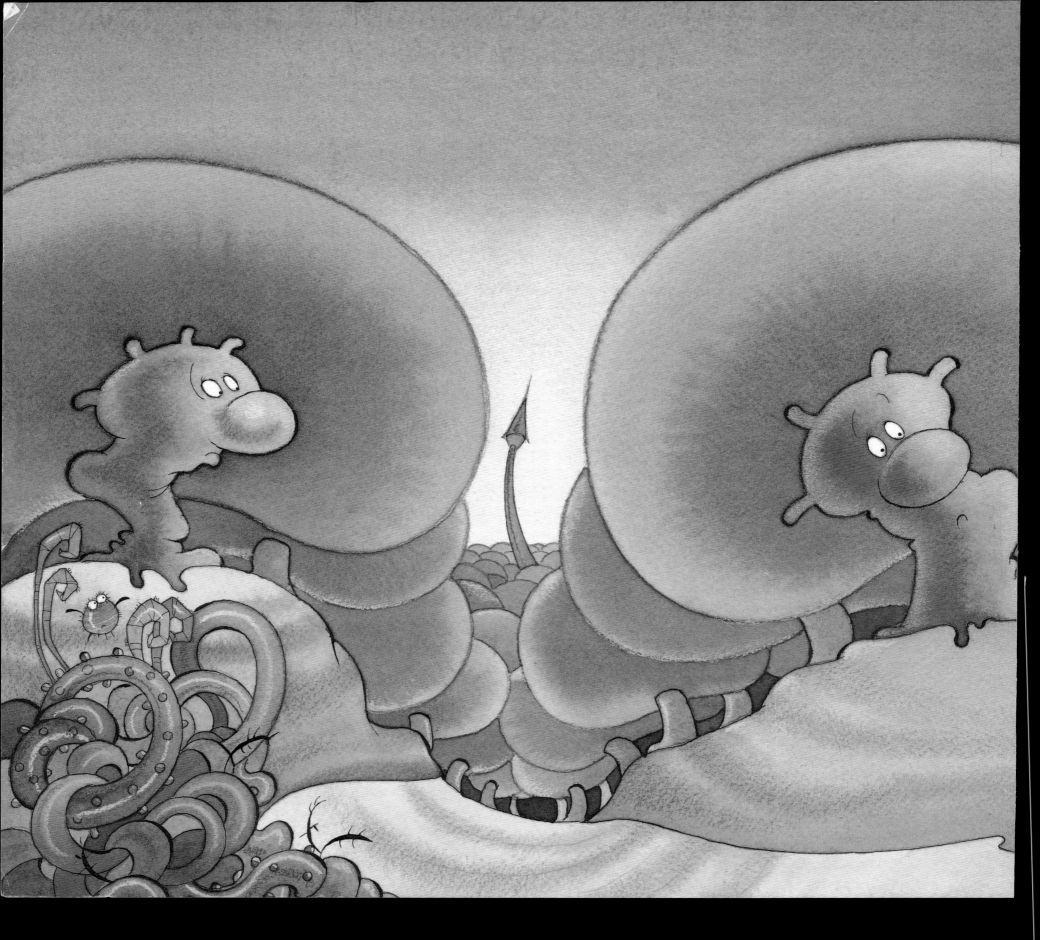

Once upon a winding path,

a wizard made his way

from a tall, tall tower with a pointy roof

to a castle on top of a hill.

"I've heard a rumour," said the
wizard to the king, "that a legendary
knight is here. A hero of old, who I've
been told, has helped dragons,

monsters,

princesses and . . .

kings.

If the rumour is right
then he's the *perfect* knight
to do a little something for *me*.

Hee hee."

The king of
the castle
scuttled off
to fetch . . .

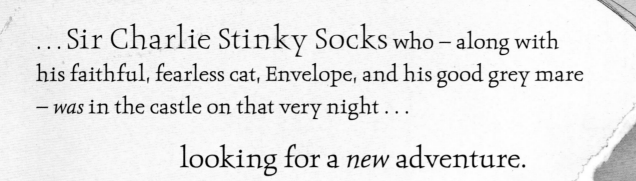

...Sir Charlie Stinky Socks who – along with his faithful, fearless cat, Envelope, and his good grey mare – *was* in the castle on that very night . . .

looking for a *new* adventure.

"Listen well," said the wizard, "here's what I need you to do.

Take a treacherous track, to a **spooky-wooky wood**, and look for a **deep, dark cave**.

Inside the cave is a little black sack, tied with a silver string.

Bring that sack back to me," he said,

"but . . .

DO NOT look inside."

Sir Charlie could hardly contain his excitement –
unlike the cat and the horse!
So off he went to bring back
the sack while . . .

. . . the wizard
sent out a
whisper.

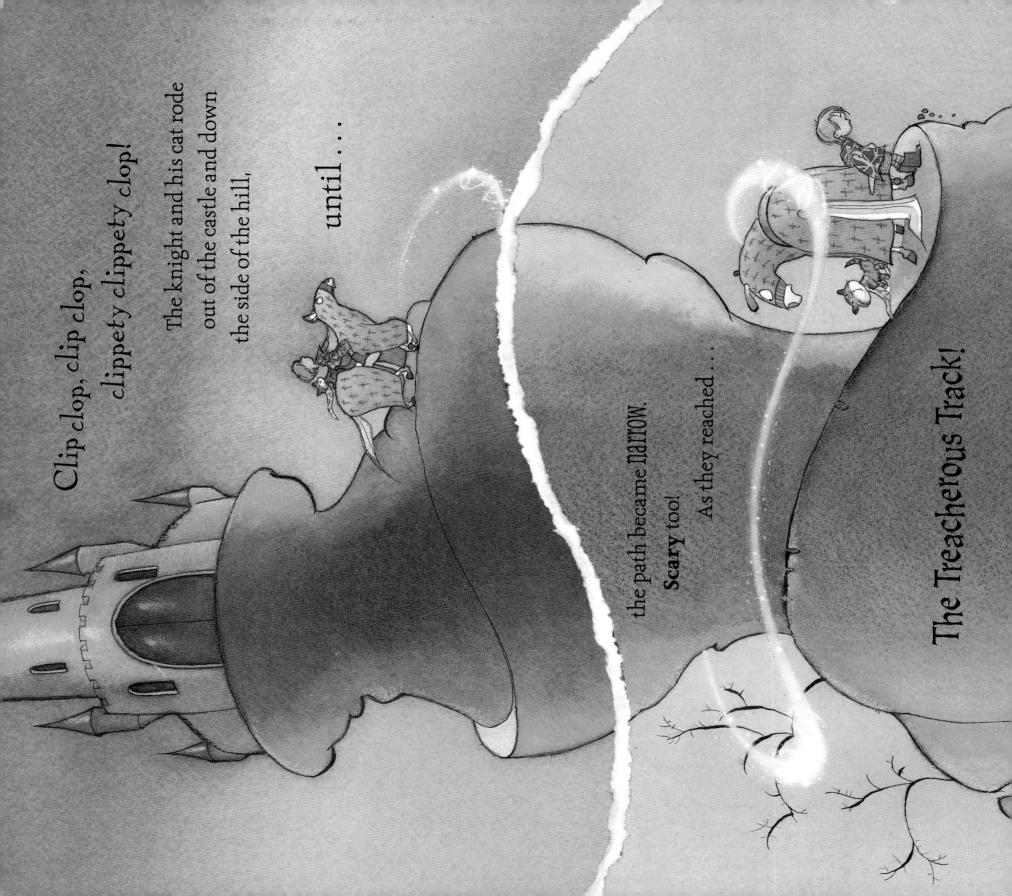

Clip clop, clip clop,
clippety clippety clop!

The knight and his cat rode
out of the castle and down
the side of the hill,

until . . . .

the path became narrow.
Scary too!
As they reached . . . .

The Treacherous Track!

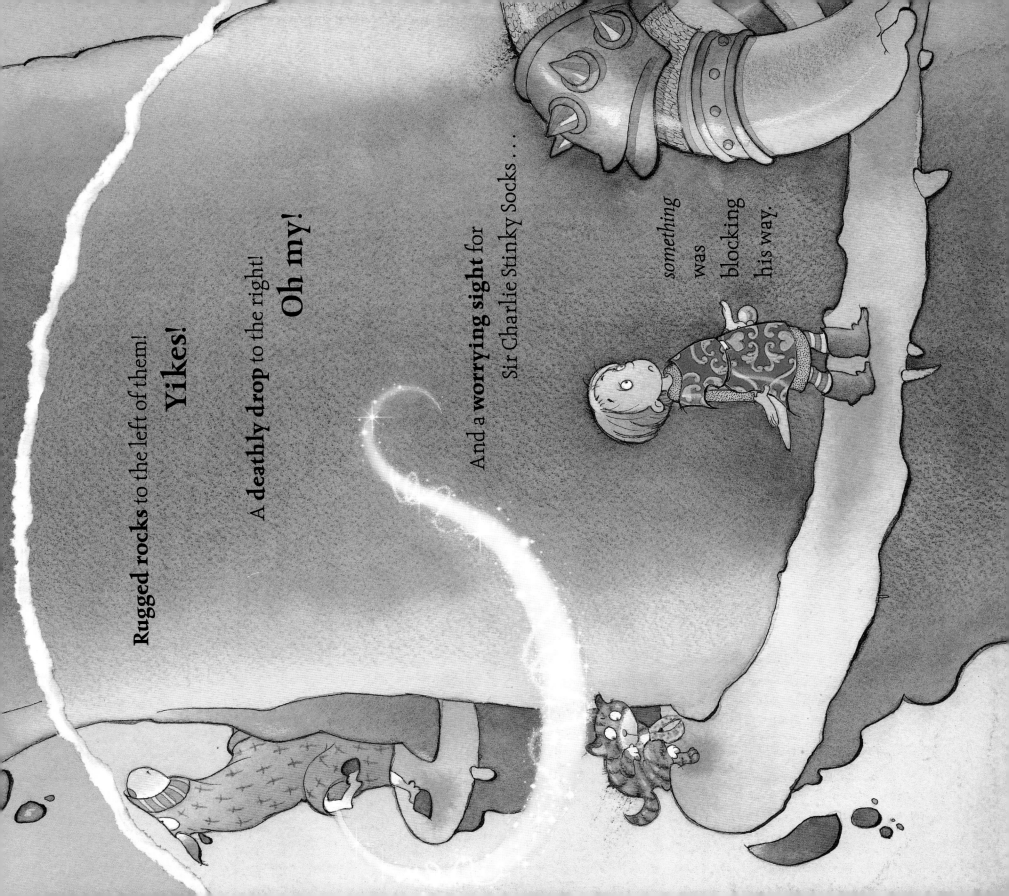

Rugged rocks to the left of them! **Yikes!**

A deathly drop to the right! **Oh my!**

And a **worrying sight** for Sir Charlie Stinky Socks . . .

something was blocking his way.

No point asking the quaking cat, Envelope.
Or the shaking grey mare.

Standing this close to a **frowning ogre**
was more than *they* could bear.

Envelope fainted!

So did the horse!

Only the wizard's whisper watched . . .

while the clever knight came up with
a plan to conquer this miserable foe.

Sir Charlie
took hold of the grey mare's tail and he . . .

The wizard's whisper spoke to the ogre . . .

. . . then carried on its way.

"You are indeed a legendary knight," laughed the **happy ogre**. "Go! Look for that sack and take it back to the castle on top of the hill."

"I will," said Sir Charlie, waking the cat and gently shaking the mare, and wondering *how on earth* the **ogre** knew where he was going.

Clip clop, clip clop!

Down to the bottom of the hill.

THAT WAY

THIS WAY

Where some **worrying signs** showed
the knight and his friends . . .

. . . the **spooky-wooky wood!**

Whoooooo!

Envelope gulped!
The grey mare gasped!
But Sir Charlie gave a grin.

"Great place to look
for a cave!"
he said.

And he led
the others in.

Shifting shadows to the left of them. **Yikes!**

A sh . . . sh . . . shuddery shape to the right. **Oh my!**

And a **worrying sight** for the knight
when he saw . . .

the cat and the horse were running as quick as they could
through that **spooky-wooky wood** – and right into . . .

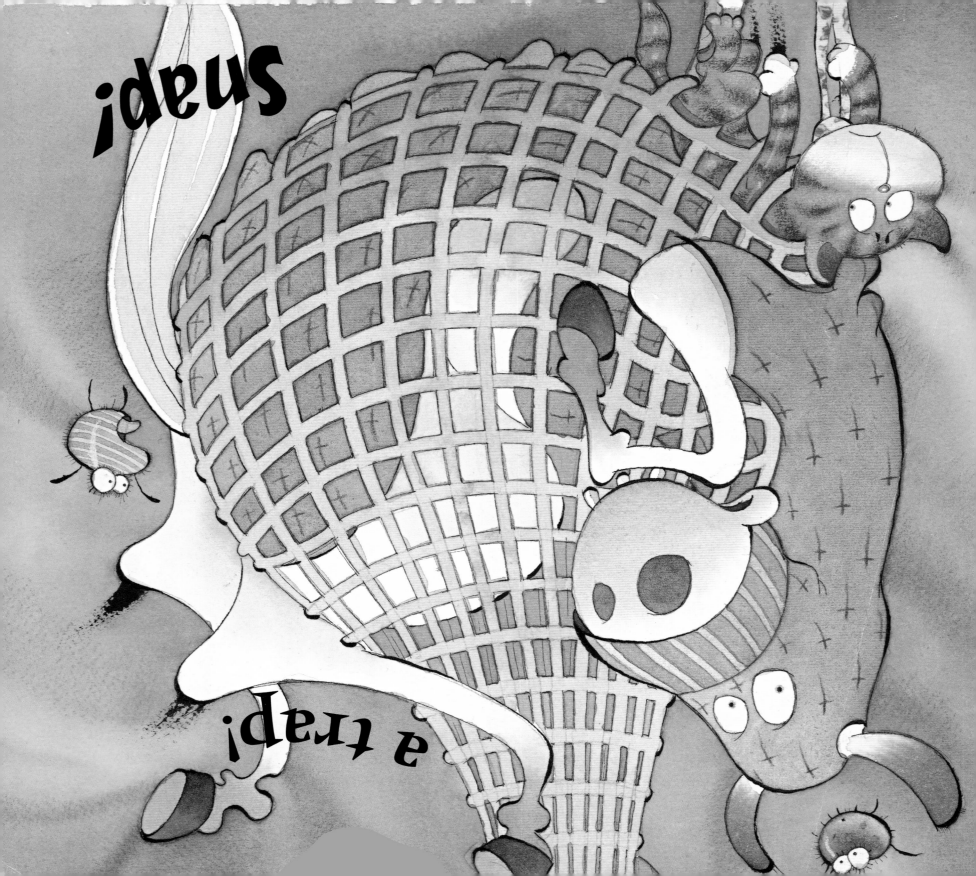

Lucky for the cat and the dangling mare,
Sir Charlie was close behind and, with
one quick flick of his trusty sword,
he set the prisoners free.

Thump!

Down on the ground,
they were safe and
sound, and . . .

. . . totally surrounded!

A scurry of SCALLYWAGS had been lying in wait
to ambush the legendary knight.

"Give us your socks!"
they shouted, "so we can
be knights like you."

Ooooooooh!

"Hold your horses!" Sir Charlie replied.
"The knight thing
was *my* idea.
Besides . . .

I've only got one pair of socks and there are loads of you.
Why don't you think of something else?
Something *all* of you can do?

What you need," said the brilliant knight, "is . . .

. . . a little imagination."

And with hankies, sticks and a few little tricks
the SCALLYWAGS pretended to be . . .

pilfering **pirates** with cutlasses,
playing among the trees.

The wizard's whisper spoke to the pirates before wending on its way.

"You are indeed a helpful knight," the **pirates** called to Sir Charlie. "Go! Find that sack and get it back to the castle on top of the hill."

"I will," said Sir Charlie, not stopping to ask *how they knew* where he was going.

Because there, where the pirates had cleared the decks, was the entrance to a cave.

Trip trap, trip trap, tippety tippety toe.

It was dismal and damp in the **deep**, **dark cave** and the trio were . . .
not alone.

From the back of the cave came snuffles
and grunts and the fearful sound of

mOOOaaaaning.

Well . . .
Envelope didn't think much of this,
nor did the good grey mare.

But at least the pair had
Sir Charlie with them
when they faced . . .

The cat fell flat on the floor again
in front of the good grey mare.

The thought of being cooked alive by this crone
was more than *they* could bear.

But bold Sir Charlie did not shiver.
Brave Sir Charlie did not shake.
He stood his ground.
He looked around.
And what did the wise knight see?

A **damp** cave.
Two **red eyes**.
Snuffles, grunts and . . . **moans.**

.... the red-eyed crone.

Lotions and potions and bunches of herbs
hung about her head and a big black
cooking pot was waiting at her feet.

Eeeeek!

"You poor old thing!" said the kindly knight.

"I believe you've got a cold."

Aaaww.

Quicker than you could say *blow your nose*,
Sir Charlie lit a fire.

He used the hanging herbs to make a comforting brew.

Then he gave the **crone** his thick, warm **socks**,
because that's what a knight *should* do.

The wizard's whisper spoke to the crone then flew far away.

"You are indeed the perfect knight," the **old crone** croaked with a smile. And she handed Sir Charlie a little black sack tied with a silver string.

"Take this back to the wizard," she said.

"But DO **NOT** LOOK INSIDE!"

Envelope's job was to hold the sack while . . .

Sir Charlie kept watch for **pirates**.

But there weren't any pirates
in the **spooky-wooky wood**,

or shadows,

or
shuddering
shapes.

Not so much as a whisper wafted among the trees.

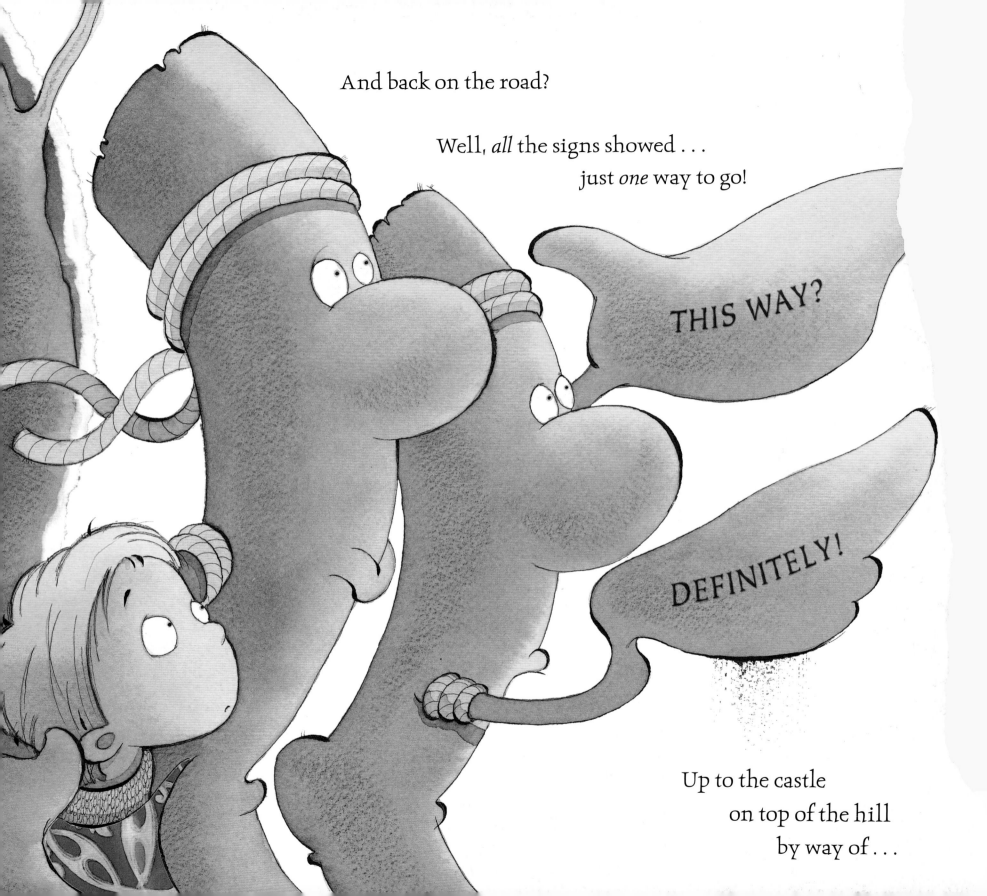

And back on the road?

Well, *all* the signs showed . . .
just *one* way to go!

THIS WAY?

DEFINITELY!

Up to the castle
on top of the hill
by way of . . .

SurP

ie had ever been kind to in all his BIG adventures
sper and gathered together
his **wonderful knight.**

There was no welcome
light in the window
that night and no one
there to greet him.

That is until . . .

Sir Charlie Stinky
Socks opened the
big wooden door.

Creeeaaaaaaak . . .

When the games had been played and the cake eaten up, the wizard remembered the sack.

"*Now* you may look inside," he said and he handed it to Sir Charlie.

The sack was a present . . .

rise!

"Don't you get it, Sir Charlie?" said the wizard,
"this time the party's . . . for YOU!"

Woo hoo!

...a new pair of socks

for

lots

more

big

adventures!

THE END